CRIME SCENE INVESTIGATION

SOLVING CRIMES WITH CHEMISTRY

BY DONNA McKINNEY

BLASTOFF! DISCOVERY

BLASTOFF! DISCOVERY, AN IMPRINT OF BELLWETHER MEDIA BY FLUTTERBEE

This edition first published in 2027 by Bellwether Media, Inc.

For information regarding permission, write to Bellwether Media, Inc., Attention: Permissions Department,
3500 American Blvd W, Suite 150, Bloomington, MN 55431.

Library of Congress Cataloging-in-Publication Data is available at www.loc.gov or upon request from the publisher.

ISBN: 9798898800833 (hardcover)
ISBN: 9798898802073 (ebook)

Editor: Rachael Barnes   Series Designer: Josh Brink

Printed in the United States of America, North Mankato, MN.

TABLE OF CONTENTS

WHAT IS FORENSIC CHEMISTRY?	4
AT THE CRIME SCENE	8
SOLVING THE CRIME	18
THE FUTURE OF FORENSIC CHEMISTRY	26
GLOSSARY	30
TO LEARN MORE	31
INDEX	32

WHAT IS FORENSIC CHEMISTRY?

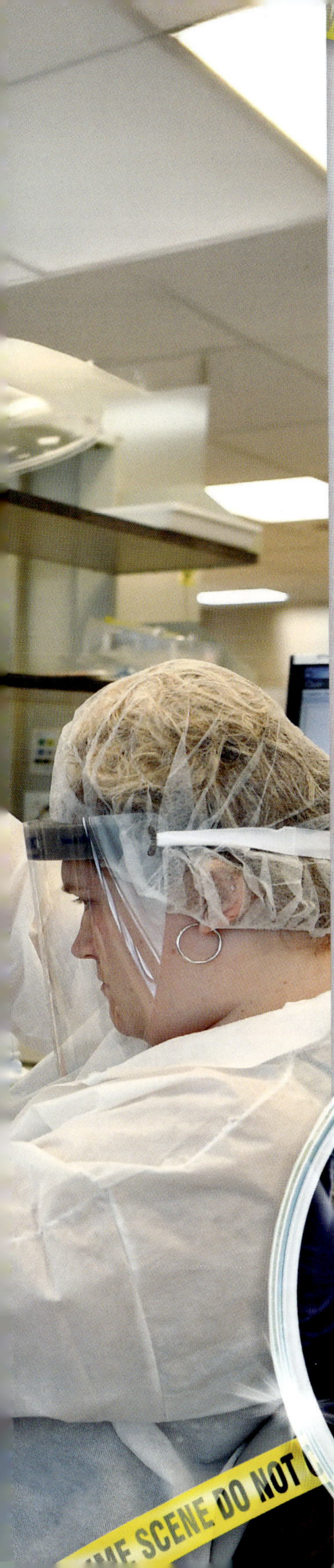

From starting a fire to scrubbing stains with soap, chemistry is in action all around! Chemistry is a field of science that deals with matter. Scientists study what matter is made of. They use tests to see how it reacts and changes.

Forensic chemistry, or the use of chemistry in crime solving, began in the 1830s. A scientist found a way to detect a certain poison in the human body. Scientists soon used this test in a murder case. The test proved the person had been killed with the poison.

A NOSE FOR CHEMISTRY

Bomb-sniffing dogs have a nose for chemistry too! They learn to detect bombs by sniffing for tiny amounts of the chemicals used to make them.

BOMB-SNIFFING DOG

Crime scene investigators (CSIs) work with **evidence** from crime scenes. Some CSI teams include **forensic scientists**. Together they search for evidence. They collect samples of different substances. Depending on the crime, they look for substances including illegal drugs, explosives, paint, glass, poisons, and blood.

Some forensic scientists are trained to run special chemical tests. They test evidence samples to identify substances. Scientists test samples such as powders, liquids, and stains. The evidence they identify helps police connect **suspects** to crimes.

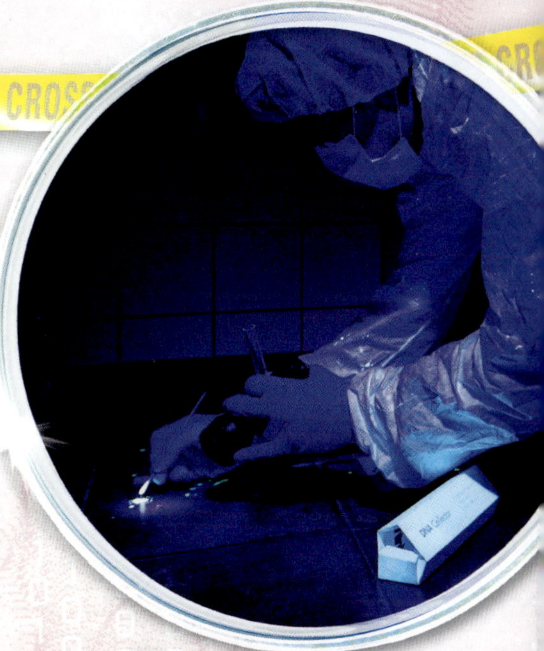

STATS

U.S. ARSON CASES

65,795 in **2024**

U.S. DRUG TRAFFICKING CASES

18,029 in **2024**

U.S. GUN DEATH CASES

14,651 in **2025**

AT THE CRIME SCENE

CSIs arrive at the crime scene quickly. It is best to collect fresh evidence. Larger police departments have CSIs on their team. In smaller departments, police are trained to collect evidence as part of their many duties.

CSIs collect crime scene **DNA** with rapid DNA tests. **DNA profiles** are created. They are sent digitally to the national DNA **database**. They are quickly compared to known DNA profiles. Rapid color tests are another portable, or easily moved, tool. They are used to test for substances such as illegal drugs, explosives, and blood. CSIs and police use these portable tests at crime scenes.

DNA TESTING

RAPID COLOR TESTS
CHEMICAL DETECTION KITS

Sometimes CSIs work on drug-related crimes. They collect drug evidence. These are illegal drugs such as cocaine, heroin, or meth. Cases can also involve **prescription drugs** being used illegally. CSIs gather the drugs and any related items. They also collect tools used to make the drugs. CSIs use portable **spectrometers** to help them learn the chemical makeup of unknown substances. They can identify substances without touching them.

CSIs may collect breath, urine, or blood samples to test for recent drug or alcohol use. Police may also collect samples from victims. Tests can show if the victims were poisoned.

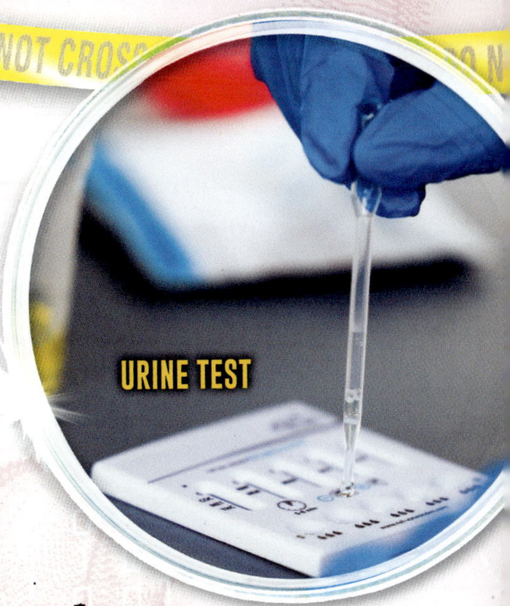

URINE TEST

CASE FILE

CRIME drug trafficking

YEAR OF THE CRIME 1989

HOW IT WAS SOLVED Police captured 20 tons of cocaine in a California warehouse. It was worth nearly $7 billion. The drug dealer planned to sell the drugs to other people. Forensic scientists proved the substance in the warehouse was cocaine. The drug dealer was sent to prison.

1989 DRUG BUST

Thousands of cases each year involve fires set on purpose to destroy property. This crime is called arson. Criminals commonly use substances called accelerants that make fires burn faster and hotter. CSIs search for accelerants used at the scene.

CSI SEARCHING FOR ACCELERANTS

CHEMISTRY AT WORK!

Chemical reactions happen every day. Rusted iron and wood burning in a fire are examples of chemical reactions!

CSIs look for burn patterns. These can show where the fire started. Burn patterns tell CSIs how the fire spread. CSIs look for matches and lighters. These might have been used to start the fire. CSIs study the evidence. They decide if the fire was set on purpose.

Some crime scenes have weapons. CSIs often find gun evidence. If they find a gun, they make sure it is unloaded. They carefully collect it. CSIs place it in a gun box. They collect bullets from the gun and the crime scene. They place these in labeled boxes or envelopes.

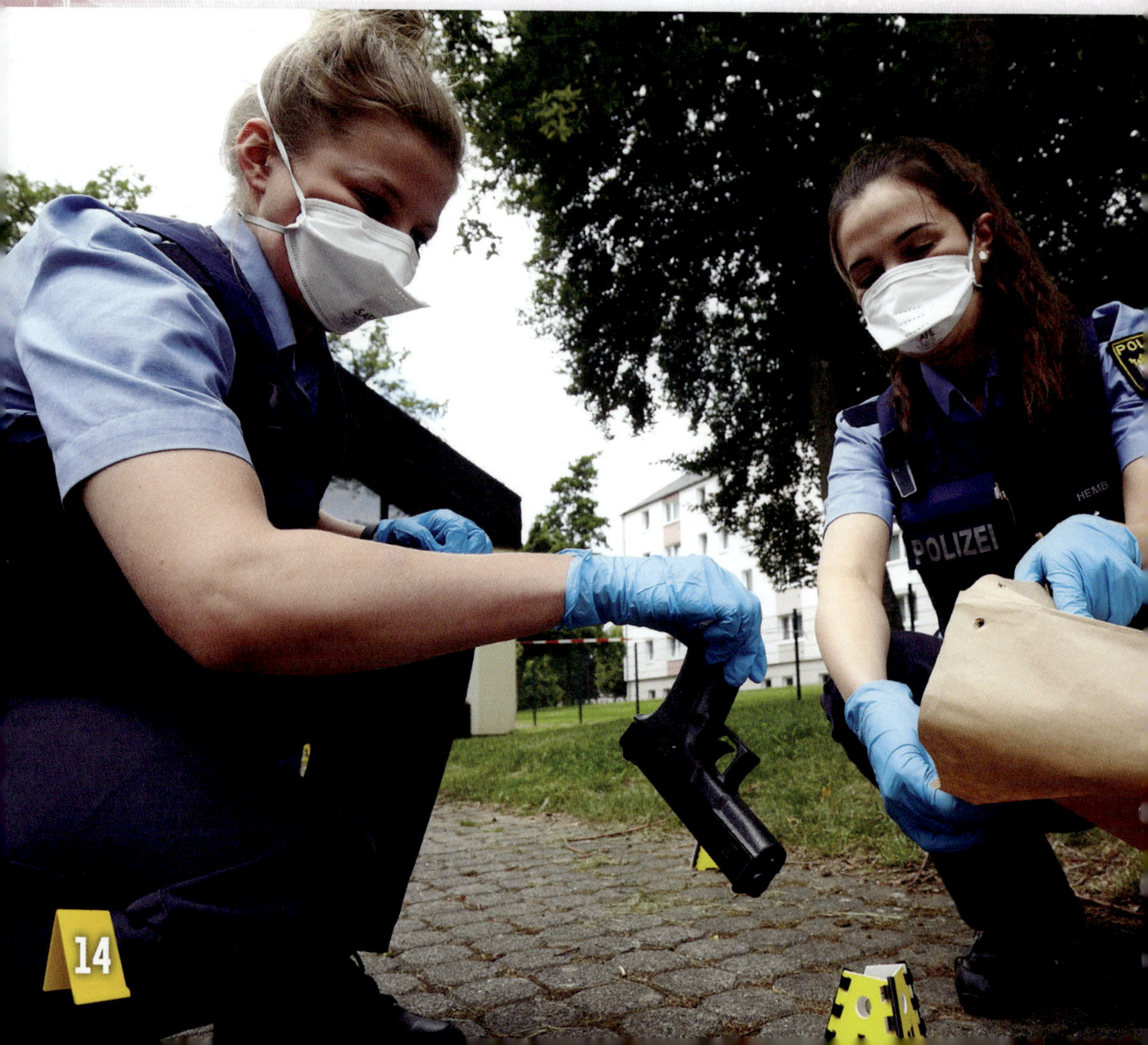

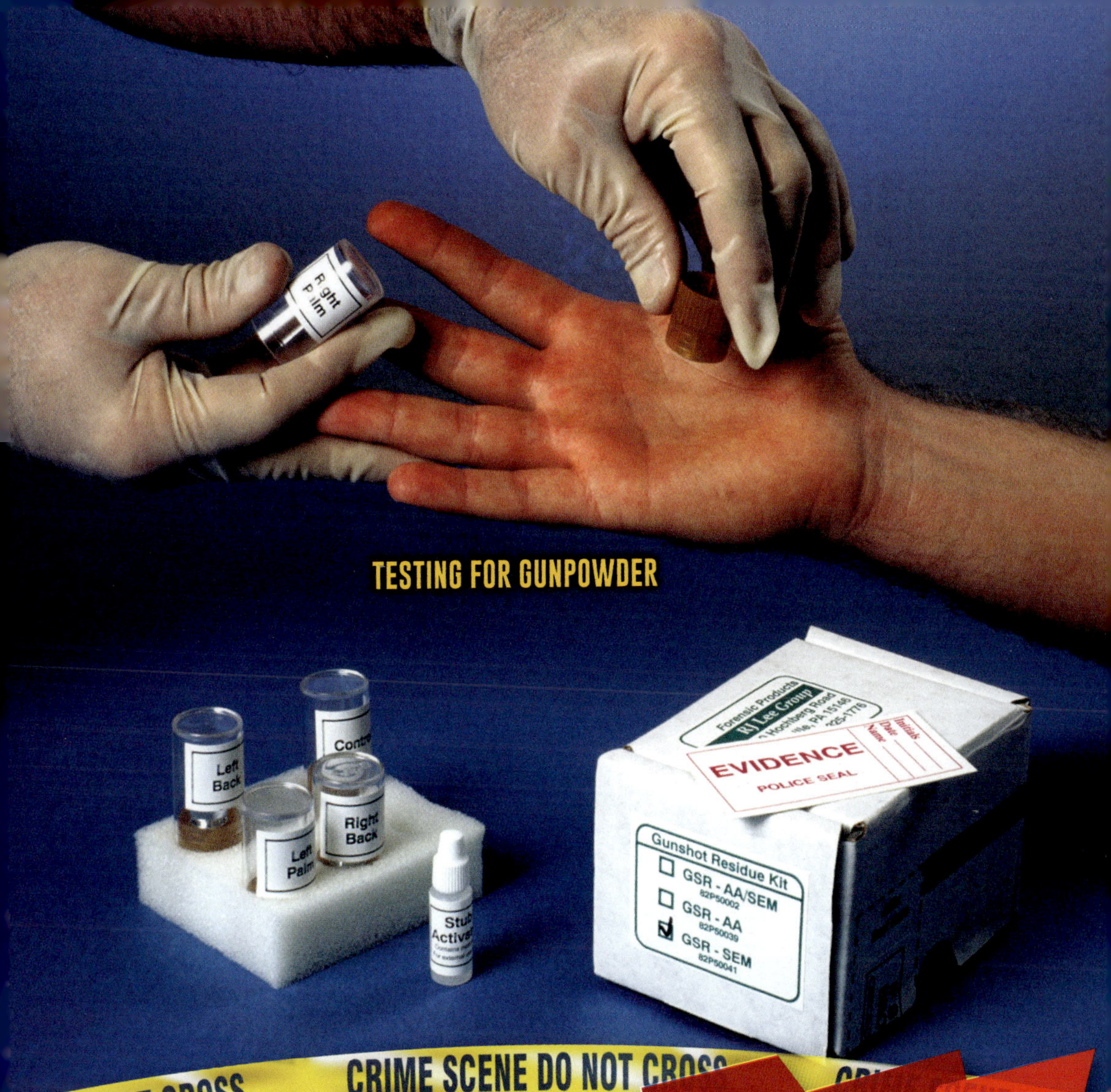

TESTING FOR GUNPOWDER

When a gun is fired, it leaves powder on skin and clothing. Gunpowder is a kind of **trace evidence**. It is not easy to see. CSIs check for powder on suspects and victims using special kits. They may use cotton swabs or tape. They also use chemicals to test for powder.

MATCHED BULLETS

Bullets are scratched when fired out of a gun. Each gun leaves unique marks. Experts study these marks to prove a weapon was used in a crime.

CSIs work with other kinds of trace evidence found at crime scenes. This includes tiny paint chips, fibers, hair, or glass. Sometimes CSIs use tweezers to collect the evidence. They scrape small sections to collect paint samples. CSIs put trace evidence in envelopes. They label them. This evidence helps link suspects to a crime scene or a victim.

CSIs search slowly. They are careful not to **contaminate** any evidence. They carefully label every piece they find.

SOLVING THE CRIME

Crime scene evidence is sent to a **forensic laboratory**, or lab. Scientists are trained to **analyze** different evidence. Scientists often begin with **presumptive testing**. These tests tell them if a substance is likely present.

Scientists review the results from the presumptive tests done at the crime scene. The first tests done at the lab are also presumptive testing. Scientists study trace evidence with **microscopes**. They also use **UV lights**. With these different tests, scientists learn which substances are present.

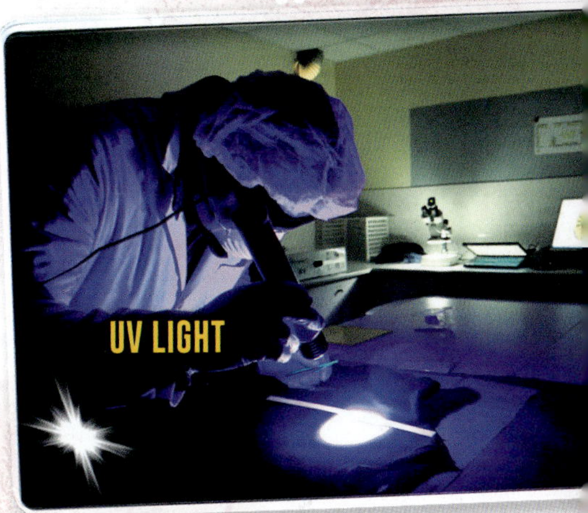

CASE FILE

CRIME letters poisoned for use as weapons

YEAR OF THE CRIME 2013

HOW IT WAS SOLVED A woman mailed letters containing a deadly substance called ricin. She sent them to people in the U.S. government. This included the president and the mayor of New York City. Forensic scientists identified the ricin using chemistry tests. The woman was caught before anyone was hurt.

Scientists put more chemistry to work with **confirmatory testing**. These tests are more accurate. They double-check the presumptive test results. Scientists identify individual parts of the substance. This lab work is usually a series of tests.

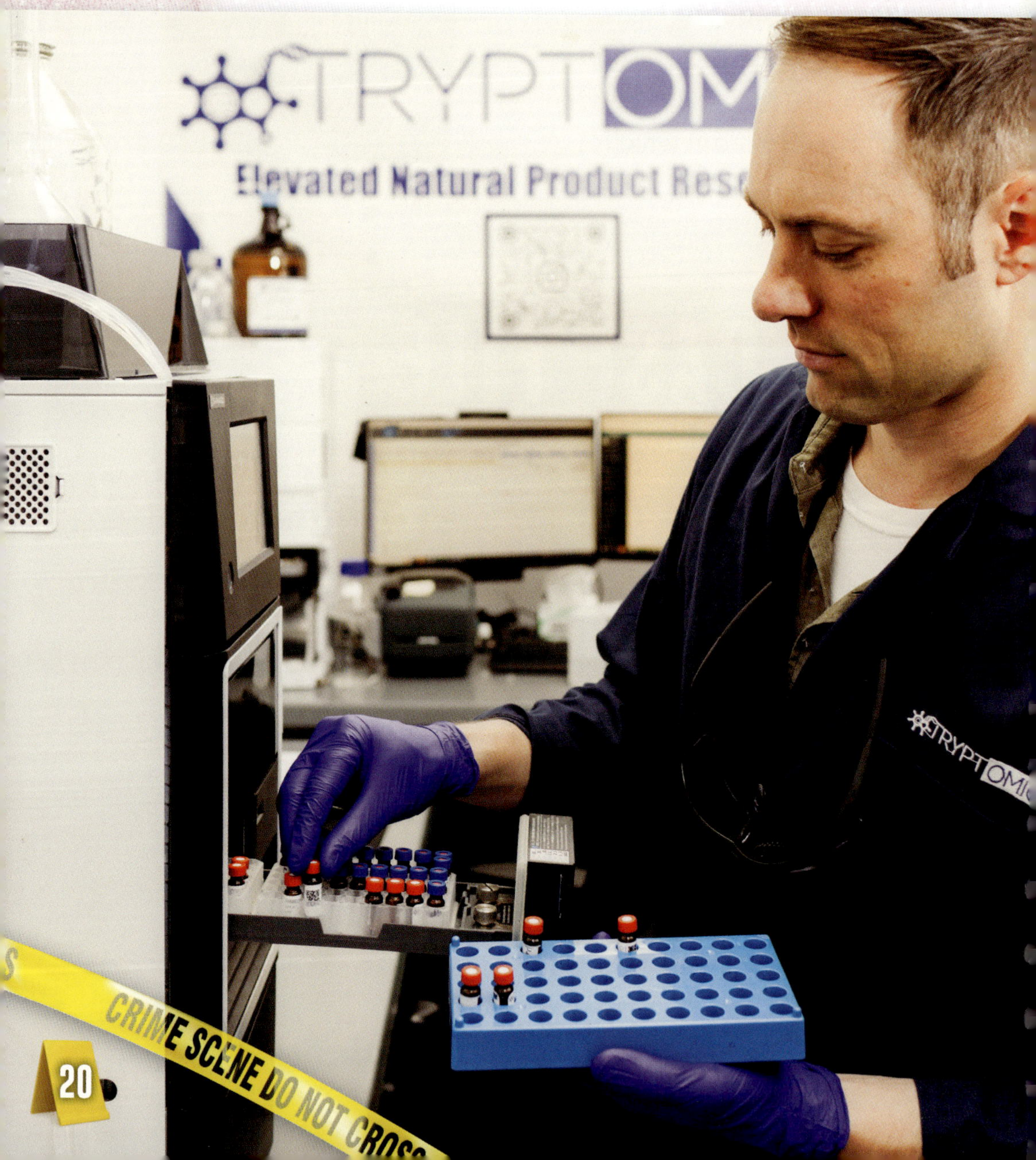

MASS SPECTROMETRY

YEAR INVENTED

invented in the **1900s**; first used for crime scene forensics in the **1950s**

HOW IT WORKS

This method is the most precise tool to identify unknown substances. Forensic labs use it to confirm trace evidence as small as a grain of sand in an Olympic-sized swimming pool. It measures the molecules in a substance. Forensic scientists use it to identify drugs, poisons, explosives, gunshot substances, and other trace evidence.

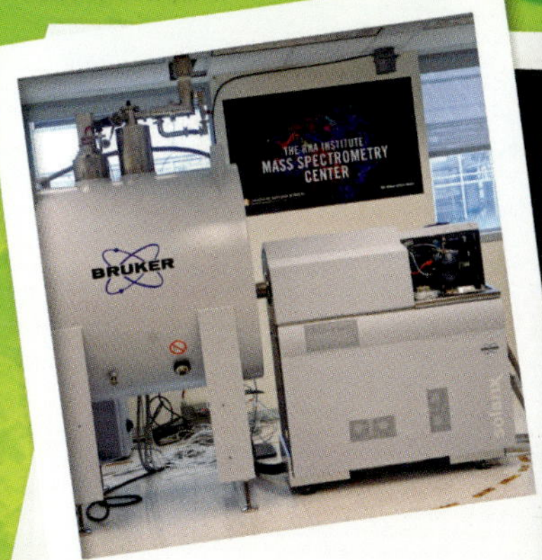

Scientists use basic chemistry along with special instruments. They use more complex methods, such as **gas chromatography**. This method separates substances. Then scientists identify each part. They do this by comparing the results to reference substances. Scientists use lab spectrometers. These help them learn the chemical makeup of the substance.

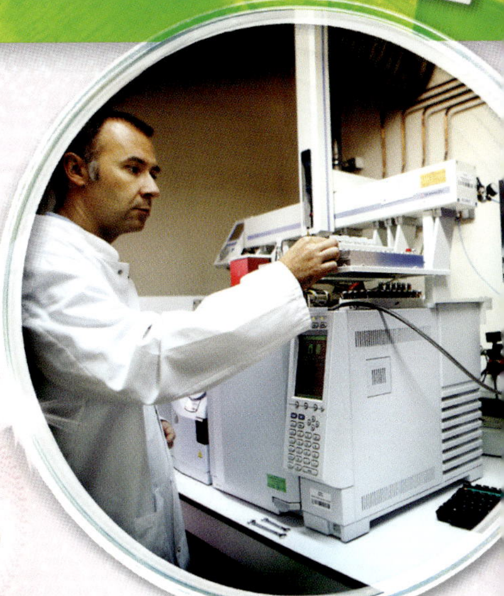

When analyzing illegal drugs, scientists can test to measure how pure the substance is. Drugs with higher purity are more dangerous to humans. In federal cases, suspects caught with higher purity drugs can get more severe punishments.

Working in the lab, a small sample can be a challenge for scientists. If there is not enough material to be tested, results might be inconclusive. Another challenge is with plant materials. This evidence can become too damaged before scientists can analyze it.

CHALLENGES

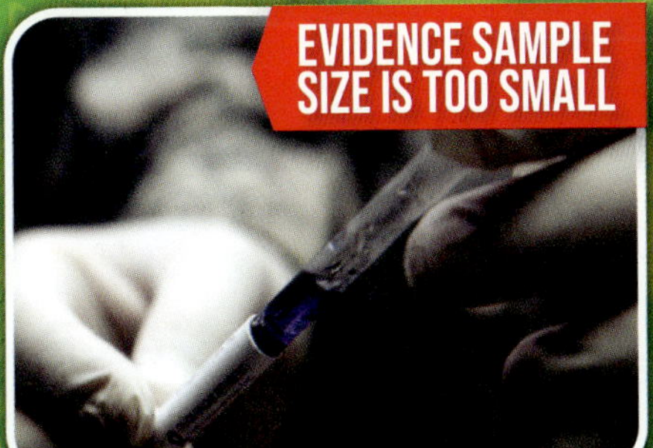

CRIME SCENE DO NOT CROSS
EXPERT WITNESS
AKG
CRIME SCENE DO NOT CROSS

Forensic labs follow strict rules. These rules apply to how scientists handle evidence. Scientists carefully document their work. They follow steps to ensure lab tools are accurate. They write detailed reports.

Scientists may serve as expert witnesses in court. They explain the tests they ran on the evidence. They describe the tools they used. They present the results in words the jury can understand. Lawyers ask questions about the evidence. Scientists who helped collect evidence may be asked about details at the crime scene. The forensic chemistry results help determine if a suspect is guilty.

THE FUTURE OF FORENSIC CHEMISTRY

Police are using new portable tools for crime scene work. Scientists now have highly sensitive portable sensors that use lasers. The sensors are used to identify separate layers of paint.

Nanosensors are another recent tool. These special sensors measure tiny amounts of dangerous substances. These include explosives, poison gases, and accelerants. These sensors are used in labs to help identify substances used in a crime. The nanosensors give a quick analysis of crime scene evidence.

FORENSIC SCIENTIST TALKING ABOUT NANOTECHNOLOGY

Artificial intelligence (AI) helps forensic scientists in their jobs. AI tools are used on DNA and trace evidence. They can quickly point to patterns in the evidence collected. These tools help scientists analyze evidence faster. They help scientists determine what evidence to test first based on data from past cases.

PROTECTING ANIMALS!

A wildlife forensic scientist uses chemistry and other sciences to solve crimes that involve plants and animals. These crimes include illegal hunting, exotic pet sales, and harmful oil spills.

Chemistry helps scientists solve crimes. It is useful at the crime scene and in the lab. Work that used to take weeks is now finished in hours. Case solved!

GLOSSARY

analyze–to look carefully at something to understand and identify its important parts

artificial intelligence–a computer's ability to do things a human mind can do

confirmatory testing–tests used to confirm the results of initial, presumptive tests

contaminate–to make something unfit to be used as evidence

crime scene investigators–people who collect and analyze evidence found at crime scenes

database–a digital system used to store and sort data

DNA–a tiny substance that carries information about the makeup of a living thing

DNA profiles–sets of DNA patterns or types that are unique to each person

evidence–a witness statement or an item or impression found at a crime scene that links a suspect to a crime

forensic laboratory–a place where scientists perform tests to study evidence left at a crime scene

forensic scientists–people who use scientific methods to study physical evidence

gas chromatography–a lab technique used to separate and identify substances in gas mixtures

microscopes–laboratory tools that make tiny things look much bigger

prescription drugs–drugs that are only given to a patient with a doctor's permission

presumptive testing–a quick test to check the possible presence of a substance

spectrometers–instruments that separate light into colors to see different wavelengths

suspects–people the police believe may have committed a crime

trace evidence–evidence that is too small to be easily seen

UV lights–ultraviolet lights used to detect blood, fingerprints, and trace evidence

TO LEARN MORE

AT THE LIBRARY

Koch, Dr. Susan Berk. *Chemical Reactions!: With 25 Science Projects for Kids*. Norwich, Vt.: Nomad Press, 2021.

McKinney, Donna. *Clues in the DNA*. Minneapolis, Minn.: Bellwether Media, 2027.

Messner, Kate, and Anne Ruppert. *Solve This! Forensics*. Washington, D.C.: National Geographic, 2020.

ON THE WEB

FACTSURFER

Factsurfer.com gives you a safe, fun way to find more information.

1. Go to www.factsurfer.com.
2. Enter "solving crimes with chemistry" into the search box and click 🔍.
3. Select your book cover to see a list of related content.

INDEX

artificial intelligence (AI), 28
case file, 11, 19
challenges, 17, 23
court, 25
crime scene investigators (CSIs), 6, 8, 9, 10, 11, 12, 13, 14, 15, 16, 17
crime scenes, 6, 8, 9, 12, 14, 16, 18, 19, 25, 26, 27, 29
evidence, 6, 7, 8, 10, 13, 14, 15, 16, 17, 18, 19, 23, 25, 27, 28
forensic laboratory, 18, 19, 20, 21, 23, 25, 27, 29
forensic scientists, 5, 6, 7, 18, 19, 20, 21, 22, 23, 25, 26, 27, 28, 29
history, 5
mass spectrometry, 21
samples, 6, 7, 11, 16, 23
stats, 7
suspects, 7, 15, 16, 22, 25
tests, 5, 7, 9, 11, 15, 18, 19, 20, 22, 23, 25
tools, 9, 10, 15, 16, 19, 21, 25, 26, 27, 28
weapons, 14, 15

The images in this book are reproduced through the courtesy of: Robert Seeberg, front cover; Jeff McCollough, pp. 2 (evidence marker 1), 3 (evidence marker 3); Uri, p. 3 (evidence marker 2); ANGELA WEISS/ AFP/ Getty Images, pp. 4-5; yacobchuk, p. 5; Gabrijelagal, p. 6; Sendo Serra/ Alamy Stock Photo, p. 6 (bottom); Couperfield, p. 7 (top); JoeDphoto, p. 7 (stats top); D-Keine, p. 7 (stats middle); Rafa Jodar, p. 7 (stats bottom); Pressmaster, p. 8; FBI media/ Federal Bureau of Investigation, pp. 9 (top), 15 (bottom), 16, 17; Obatala-photography, p. 9 (middle); Vasilii Binzari, p. 9 (bottom); BAY ISMOYO/ AFP/ Getty Images, p. 10; Christoph Reichwein/ AP Images, p. 11; CECIL YATES/ L.A DAILY NEWS/ AFP/ Getty Images, p. 11 (bottom); Tino Plunert/ dpa-Zentralbild/ ZB/ dpa/ Alamy Stock Photo, p. 12; Liam McBurney/ PA Images/ Getty Images, p. 13; Prathaan, p. 13 (bottom); Patrick van Katwijk/ Getty Images, p. 14 (top); Thomas Frey/ picture alliance/ Getty Images, p. 14 (bottom); David R. Frazier Photolibrary, Inc./ Alamy Stock Photo, p. 15; PRESSLAB, p. 17; Arne Dedert/ picture alliance/ Getty Images, p. 18; PHILIPPE HUGUEN/ AFP/ Getty Images, p. 19; Evan Lewis/ AP Images, p. 19; Joanna Kulesza for The Washington Post/ Getty Images, p. 20; Lori Van Buren/ Albany Times Union/ Getty Images, pp. 21, 27; BSIP/ Universal Images Group/ Getty Images, p. 21 (bottom); Kantele Franko/ AP Images, p. 22; Kyndell Harkness/ Minneapolis Star Tribune/ TNS/ Alamy Stock Photo, p. 23; Jack Spades/ Wikimedia Commons, p. 23 (challenges top left); andriano_cz, p. 23 (challenges top right); Sinhyu Photographer, p. 23 (challenges bottom); Patrick Seeger/ picture alliance/ Getty Images, pp. 24-25; Doug Beghtel/ AP Images, p. 25; Nick Ansell/ AP Images, p. 26; SolStock, p. 28; Monty Rakusen, p. 29.